30 ♥ DAYS TO LOVE

Daily Meditations, Inspirations & Actions for Creating a Life of Love

RHONDA SCIORTINO

30 Days to Love

Text Copyright © 2023 Rhonda Sciortino

Library of Congress Cataloging-in-Publication Data
is available.
ISBN: 978-1-57826-915-0

COVER AND INTERIOR DESIGN BY CAROLYN KASPER

Printed in the United States
10 9 8 7 6 5 4 3 2 1

This book is dedicated to everyone who has ever felt unloved, unwanted, or as though they don't belong. The good news is that you can feel loved and valued. This little book is going to show you how.

CONTENTS

INTRODUCTION

*"I expect to pass through life but once.
If, therefore, there be any kindness I can
show, or any good thing I can do to any fellow
being, let me do it now, and not defer or
neglect it, as I shall not pass this way again."*
—WILLIAM PENN

We have all felt that awful feeling of rejection, of feeling unwanted, left out, or unloved. It is a terrible feeling.

The worst part is that feeling unloved diminishes (and in some cases, destroys) our potential. Think about it: people who feel loved and valued are more confident. They are more willing to step out of their comfort zones to take risks like applying for jobs that are slightly out of their reach or asking someone who seems slightly out of their league out on a date.

People who feel loved know that even if they do not get the job or the date, they will be okay because they are loved. They know that their value is not diminished by any perceived failure.

Those who do not feel that way are less likely to take those risks because when they do not get the job or the date, they feel like losers. When they have no one encouraging them to get up, dust themselves off, and get back in the game, that feeling of being a loser seems confirmed. After they experience too many of those types of failures, they quit trying at all.

We all need someone who believes in us, who cheers us on in life. The consequences of not having at least one person in our corner is ultimately sadness, depression, and maybe even despair, which is a needlessly dismal outcome because it costs nothing to believe in someone or for someone else to believe in us.

One thing that almost all of us can agree on is how sad it is when children are abused, when families are homeless, when old people languish alone, etc. Some of us question why, if there is a

God, He would allow such things. However, what if the answer to those things is you and me? What if just the simple act of connecting with people, caring about them, and sharing what we have is what is intended for all of us?

Love heals. When we feel loved, we feel better. When we feel unloved, we feel badly. So, when we love ourselves and others, we feel better and so do the people we love.

This little book shows us HOW to love and be loved. If you put the simple tips in this book into practice in your life, you will feel better within 30 days. One act of love given or received can make a dramatic difference.

As you read through this book, there might be times when you think that it is too "others focused," and not focused enough on helping you feel love. However, the reality is that when we are giving love, we feel better. Love always splashes back up on the person who is giving it. So, even if you are tempted to throw in the towel over the next 30 days, please do not stop. If you do, you will never know how good it can feel to love and to be loved.

What have you got to lose? Whether you try this or not, thirty days from now you will be thirty days older. If you are thirty days older with love in your life, you will feel better. It really is that simple.

DAY 1
LOVE YOURSELF

"Loving yourself first doesn't make you vain or selfish—it makes you indestructible."

—Anonymous

Love yourself! Many people hope to find someone to love and who will love them. The first step to finding the right person is to love yourself. Yes, that is right. It sounds counterintuitive, but it is true.

Think about it. People are attracted to people who are loving and kind. So, if we want to attract the right people into our lives, we need to act like the kind of people we want in our lives. We must be willing and ready to love and to receive love.

The challenge is that many of us do not love ourselves. Some of us do not even really like ourselves. When asked to describe ourselves, most of us start off with a long list of all the things that we wish were different or that we would like to change. We talk about what we do for a living or about our family or where we're from, but rarely do we meet a person who rattles off a long list of all the awesome things about themselves! Most of us would find that extremely awkward. We avoid anything that sounds boastful or that could be perceived as arrogant.

There is nothing wrong with liking ourselves and having love for ourselves. How can we expect anyone else to love us if we do not think that there is anything lovable about us? The truth is that we are lovable, and it is not arrogant to believe that!

You cannot expect someone else to come along and give you love when you are not willing to love yourself, and you cannot give love to anyone else if you have none in your heart. You cannot give what you do not have, so if you want to give love to others, the logical place to start is in loving yourself.

It does not matter who should have loved you but did not, or who let you down, or whether or not anyone has ever loved you. Know this:

You are worthy

You are lovable

You are awesome

You are full of good character traits, personality traits, abilities, strengths and natural talents. Do not forget that you have a unique perspective that has been formed by all of your life experiences. You have wisdom that others do not have because of your life experiences. Do not dismiss any of these things as no big deal, assuming that everyone has them. Everyone does not have the combination of the things you have that make you unique in all the world.

"Love yourself enough to set boundaries.
Your time and energy are precious.
You get to choose how you use it. You teach
people how to treat you by deciding
what you will and won't accept."
—Anna Taylor

Meditation

I am worthy. I am lovable. I am unique in all the world. I am awesome.

Action

- I will list my best character traits, like resilience, resourcefulness, or patience.

- I will list my best personality traits, like being a good listener, being a good friend, or being trustworthy.

- I will list some of the things that I know how to do, like cook, fix things, or encourage others.

Regardless of what you think is wrong with you, or what you think you lack, remember always that you are "FLAWSOME," which means that you are someone who acknowledges their "flaws" and recognizes that they are awesome regardless!

On a scale of 1–10, 10 being highest, how would you rate your love for yourself? How will you increase your score?

DAY 2

LOVE THOSE CLOSEST TO YOU

"Never worry about numbers. Help one person at a time and always start with the person nearest you."
—Saint Teresa of Calcutta

Love those closest to you. Let's be honest, sometimes it is most difficult to love the people who are closest to us. These are the people who we see at their worst. We see them when they are tired, grouchy, anxious, and ill.

When people show us the worst sides of themselves, it is because they trust us. They trust that we are not going to judge them or hurt them or leave them because they are not at their best. That may be nice, but it does not make it any easier to deal with them during those difficult times. At these times, it is most important to love those who are closest to us.

It is easy to say things like, "I'll always be there for you" when everything is great. It is much more difficult to actually follow through and be there when people are going through a rough patch.

Likewise, it is easy to be patient with people when they are behaving well. It is effortless to be forgiving when others are not doing anything wrong. It is when people are being difficult that we really need to make the effort to love them.

If you want to make love the core of your character and the central theme of your life and live the beautiful life that is borne out of that commitment, then prepare yourself to show love regardless of how others are behaving.

We talked on Day 1 about the importance of loving yourself. This is our starting point for a reason. You cannot fully love others until you care for yourself. Caring for yourself includes making the decision that you will not take offense when others are being difficult. You can decide to erect an invisible wall around your heart that deflects insults that can fly out of the mouths of people who are not at their best.

If the difficult person is not able to be the loving, caring person you need, consider a greater level of self-care during difficult times, or talk to a friend, pastor, or counselor. It is important to remember that no one person can ever meet all of our emotional needs. That is too much pressure on a person, and frankly, it is giving others too much power over us.

"Patience is not the ability to wait, but the ability to keep a good attitude while waiting."
—Anonymous

Meditation

I am kind. I am patient. I do not take things personally.

Action

- I will find people I can safely talk to when I need help meeting my emotional needs.

- I will ignore hurtful things that are said when those closest to me are not at their best.

- I will not allow the irritability of others to affect my mood or behavior.

Sometimes the toughest people to love are those who are closest to us, but you can do this! You can be kind and loving regardless of what other people do. And when you refuse to let the poor behavior of others affect your attitude, you are modeling for everyone within your influence how to love those who are closest to you!

On a scale of 1–10, 10 being highest, how would you rate your ability to love those closest to you? How will you increase your score?

DAY 3
ACTS OF SERVICE

"Great opportunities are often disguised as small acts of service."
—RICK WARREN

A cts of service are some of the easiest and most meaningful ways of giving love to another.

Acts of service can be just about anything that you are able to do for someone. It is your way of literally demonstrating kindness toward another person. For someone who enjoys cooking or baking, it could be making a little extra and taking a meal or a plate of cookies to someone. It could be giving someone a ride to work whose car is in the shop. It could be as simple as holding the door open for someone.

Acts of service are important because while other ways of showing love might be too subtle for some people to recognize, an act of service is out there in the world for others to see.

Acts of service set a terrific example for everyone in our life—especially the young people. When others see us showing love through acts of service, they are literally learning how to live a life of loving kindness.

When we make giving acts of service to others a lifestyle, we may not ever have to say a word about it to the people in our lives to whom we would like to pass on our values. Our actions speak loudly and can easily be adopted by others because they have personally seen our demonstrations of love in action. Others are far more likely to follow in our ways when they see our demonstration of acts of service rather than listening to our lectures.

Consider the ways that you have shown acts of service to others. How were those actions received?

It is human nature to pull back from people who did not acknowledge or appreciate our acts of service. Conversely, it is easier to do more for people who are appreciative and grateful for our acts of service. It is especially gratifying to exchange acts of service with those who do their best to reciprocate.

Although it is wonderful when someone reciprocates, it is important that we remember that a true act of service, done in love, is never given for the purpose of receiving something in return. Authentic love is never quid-pro-quo, a trade of one thing for another. Real, authentic love, not a cheap counterfeit, is what we all want in our lives. It is always given with no expectations at all. Although it feels great when someone acknowledges our acts of service, it is important that we do them with no expectation of anything in return, including even the simplest of acknowledgements.

The reason this is so important is that expecting something that never comes destroys our own gratification about the act of service we have given. Whereas when we drop any expectation, we can feel good about the good we have done simply for the sake of doing good and being a good person.

When we can rely on our own internal barometer about our goodness, kindness, and love, without expecting anyone else to acknowledge us, we are in control of our happiness.

"God uses millions of no-name influencers every day in the simplest selfless acts of service. They are the teachers whose names will never be in the newspaper, pastors who will never author a book, managers who will never be profiled in a magazine, artists whose work is buried in layers of collaboration, writers whose sphere of influence is a few dozen people who read their blogs. But they are the army that makes things happen. To them devotion is its own reward. For them influence is a continual act of giving, nothing more complicated than that."

—MEL LAWRENZ

Meditation

I am about service to others.

Action

- I will find ways to be of service to someone today and every day.

- I will not expect anything in return for the acts of service that I freely give.

- I will set an example for everyone within my influence for living a life of love through acts of service to others.

Your acts of service to the people in your life may be common, everyday acts of service, but they may also be things that you are uniquely able to do. For example, you may be able to show someone how to do something that most people do not know how to do. You may be able to share a bit of knowledge or a skill that is not commonly found. Whatever act of service you provide, rest in the knowledge that your act of service is a contribution that makes the world a better place!

On a scale of 1–10, 10 being highest, how would you rate your acts of service? How will you increase your score?

DAY 4

CHEER UP SOMEONE

"The unselfish effort to bring cheer to others will be the beginning of a happier life for ourselves."
—HELEN KELLER

B ring good cheer. One of the best ways to show love is to attempt to cheer up someone who is down. We all feel down from time to time, and regardless of whether we are feeling low over a serious situation that no one can change, or we are simply having a bad day, it is comforting when someone makes the attempt to cheer us up.

We can do it with a word of encouragement, an unexpected hot cup of coffee that shows up on our desk, a handwritten note, or even a joke.

Sometimes it does not matter what the actual action is, but rather it is the fact that someone cared enough to take time out of their day to make the attempt.

We do not need to wait until someone is down to bring good cheer. We can be the people who brighten every room we enter. We can decide to be the people who have a perpetually good attitude.

Contrary to the opinions of some (who, coincidentally, tend to have perpetually bad attitudes), our attitudes are a choice that we make. Human beings are capable of having full control of our attitudes. Regardless of our circumstances, we can decide to have a good attitude. We do not have to allow ourselves to be slaves to our circumstances. This deliberate choice of attitudes can be found in the life of Viktor Frankl, an Austrian psychiatrist and Holocaust survivor, who intentionally maintained control of his attitude while a prisoner in Nazi concentration camps. Dr. Frankl said, "Everything can be taken from a man but one thing: the last of the human freedoms—to choose one's attitude in any given set of circumstances, to choose one's own way."

So, despite whatever challenges you may be facing, look for people to whom you can bring cheer, and deliberately think of ways you can do it. Some simple ideas are to find a daily calendar of jokes or funny anecdotes and be ready to share them with others; get a bag of individually wrapped mints or candies and share them with everyone you meet. Call, text, or email something cute or funny to someone. The little-known secret is that when we make others feel better, we tend to feel better.

Turning our attention to someone else gets our mind off of our own challenges. The great news is that sometimes moving our focus off of our problems allows us to see them in a different perspective when we return to them. Oftentimes, when we see a challenge in a different light, we are better able to see the opportunity beneath the challenge. Ideas are more likely to form in a cool, clear mind that is not tangled up in heated thoughts about the problem and its ramifications.

> *"The best way to cheer yourself up is to try to cheer somebody else up."*
> —MARK TWAIN

Meditation

I look for ways to cheer up everyone within my influence.

Action

- I will find humorous comics or stories to share when opportunities to do so arise.

- I will always be ready with a word of encouragement.

- I will keep a smile on my face and maintain a positive mental attitude so that my smile and attitude will become contagious.

When you make cheering up others a lifestyle, your smiling face and cheerful attitude will encourage others. Just imagine it, your very presence will uplift others!

On a scale of 1–10, 10 being highest, how would you rate your ability to cheer up others? How will you increase your score?

DAY 5
CARE

"We live in a world in which we need to share responsibility. It's easy to say, 'It's not my child, not my community, not my world, not my problem.' Then there are those who see the need and respond. I consider those people my heroes."

—FRED ROGERS

C are about others. If you are a naturally caring person, you may find the idea of an entire day of this 30 days to love challenge being dedicated to caring about others unnecessary. If it is your nature to care about others, you may be surprised to learn that many people go through their lives so inwardly focused that they have no idea what others are going through. Sadly, these people usually don't care to find out about the struggles of others.

Many of us are facing enormous challenges ourselves, and we simply do not have the capacity to deal with our situations plus care about others. Others of us are so busy with our lives that we fail to turn our attention away from our busy schedule to look into the eyes of others who we encounter throughout our days.

The good news is that genuinely caring about others actually enriches our own lives. The act of turning our attention away from ourselves for a time, creates perspective and context for the things we deal with in our own lives. When we notice what others are experiencing, we often find that our own problems are not nearly as dire as we first believed. Another benefit is that we may find ourselves learning from others. We learn from others who have already dealt with the challenges we are facing. We may find ourselves inspired by the ways that others deal with their problems.

Although the average person in the US lives nearly 80 years, the reality is that that eight decades fly by rapidly. The faster the pace of our lives, the faster those years pass. For many of us, those years become blurred chunks of time that are delineated by the times in our lives when we looked up and noticed another. These are the life experiences that stand out in a well lived life. These are the times when we met the person who would become our closest friend, the time we met our spouse, the times the children in our lives were born, and so on.

When we pause long enough to consider the most important times of our lives, we often find that the times that meant the most to us are the times that we most cared about others.

Let yourself care without making your care conditioned on whether the other person cares about you. The people you choose to care about may not have the capacity to care about you. That is okay. Just like with every other aspect of love, caring does not have to be given in exchange for returned care and concern. We will attract people who will care about us when we seek nothing in return.

"As human beings we each have a responsibility to care for humanity. Expressing concern for others brings inner strength and deep satisfaction. As social animals, human beings need friendship, but friendship doesn't come from wealth and power, but from showing compassion and concern for others."

—THE DALAI LAMA

Meditation

I am not concerned only with myself. I care about others.

Action

- I will deliberately stop what I am doing today and think about, and care about, others.

- I will remind myself that there are others who live with greater challenges than I do.

- I will not limit my concern to only those in my inner circle. I care about the plight of others I may never meet.

A caring heart is a loving heart. The more you intentionally care about others, the more concern for humanity that you will develop. While you cannot solve the problems of others, your awareness and concern keep your life in perspective and your heart tenderized.

On a scale of 1–10, 10 being highest, how would you rate your care and concern for others? How will you increase your score?

DAY 6
SHOW COMPASSION

"To be successful is to be helpful, caring and constructive, to make everything and everyone you touch a little bit better."
—DR. NORMAN VINCENT PEALE

Show compassion to others, regardless of their political affiliation, religious beliefs (or lack thereof), socio-economic status, race, gender, or any of the other ways that we divvy ourselves up.

It seems as though we live in a world in which some people notice the presidential candidate bumper stick on the back of the mangled car and decide not to stop and help the people trapped inside. We can replace the presidential candidate sticker with a religious symbol or the logo or symbol of a particular group or simply the color of the skin of the people inside the vehicle and find the same lack of compassion toward other human beings.

It is not authentic compassion to only help people who are like us or with whom we agree. This would be like parents who say they love their child, but when they hear the child screaming for help from outside, stop to check the child's grades before deciding whether to run outside to help the child.

In the same way, it is not compassion to stop and help someone because they happen to be popular and can reciprocate by helping you get more likes on your social media page. It is also not real compassion to stop what you are doing to help the CEO of the company you work for in order to garner favor of the person at the top.

Let's hope it hasn't come to only showing compassion to the people we believe deserve it or with whom we can expect something in return, but given the vitriol and villainization of "the others," it wouldn't be surprising to learn that many people have drawn subtle lines around where, when, and to whom they will show compassion.

Now imagine a world in which we disregard all social identifiers before rushing to the aid of another. Helping someone regardless of the ways in which they are different from us is the definition of true compassion. True, authentic compassion is the only real compassion.

Real compassion is blind to our divisions and is concerned only with the fact that another human being needs help, help that we are able to provide. Whether that help is to dive in and do what is necessary to bring relief to the person who is suffering or simply to stop what we're doing and call someone who can, the act of love is to run with reckless abandon toward the person who is hurting without regard for differences or for what we hope for in return.

"Compassion asks us to go where it hurts, to enter into the places of pain, to share in brokenness, fear, confusion, and anguish. Compassion challenges us to cry out with those in misery, to mourn with those who are lonely, to weep with those in tears. Compassion

requires us to be weak with the weak, vulnerable with the vulnerable, and powerless with the powerless. Compassion means full immersion in the condition of being human."

—HENRI NOUWEN

Meditation

I show compassion for others regardless of our differences.

Action

- I will be aware of people who are suffering so that I may show compassion.

- I will not turn a blind eye to the suffering of others regardless of who they are or how different they may be from me.

- I will take the time to do what I am able to do to show authentic compassion to others.

Compassion, when turned into action, is evidence of maturity. It is also a meaningful demonstration of the love in our hearts. This is especially true when we show compassion toward people who are outside of our inner circle of family and close friends.

On a scale of 1–10, 10 being highest, how would you rate your compassion for the suffering of others? How will you increase your score?

DAY 7
LISTEN

"The first duty of love is to listen."
—Paul Tillich

listen to others. One of the easiest ways to get to know someone, really know them, and to show that you genuinely care is to listen to them without interruption.

In our fast-paced culture, we often do not take the time to really stop, turn our attention to another, and listen to what they are saying. So many problems with relationships could be improved if only we would truly listen.

The International Coaching Federation talks about three different levels of listening. Many of us live our entire lives at Level 1 listening, which is where we listen to others, but as we do, we are thinking about how what is said relates to our own thoughts, opinions, judgments, and feelings. It is as though we take in the words of another and fit them into our perspective or reject them because they do not fit into our perspective.

Worse still, some of us are forming our "comeback lines" or focusing on the sting of the perceived insult we just heard while listening to others. We are thinking more about what we are going to say than about what the speaker in front of us is saying. When this is the case, we are really not listening to what the other person is saying.

We think we are listening because we think we can do both listening and thinking at the same time; however, research suggests that our brains are not nearly as good at handling multiple tasks as we think they are. Our brains do not actually process both thoughts at once. Rather, our brains shift back and forth, meaning that we are missing entire sentences from the other person while our brain is focused on our feelings or on how we are planning to respond.

It is not difficult to imagine how this, the most common level of listening, results in beaks in relationships.

One of the single most effective ways to truly show love is to learn how to listen to hear others. This means really focusing on what the other person is saying while ignoring distractions. Level 2 listening is being totally focused on the other person. Some examples of times that most of us have listened intently to really hear another person are when a potential employer is about to give us the news of whether they have decided to hire us for a job we desperately want. Another is when we have asked someone to marry us or we're the one being asked. Another might be the last whispered words of a loved one on his or her deathbed.

In these types of situations, we tune out the noise around us and lean in, sometimes straining to hear what the other person is saying. We do that instinctively because we genuinely care about what the other person is saying. These words can change our lives, so we intuitively want to hear not only the words themselves, but the way they are spoken, the intonation, the inferences, and the implications. These words have meaning to us.

If we were to listen to every conversation like we listen to the most important ones, we would be communicating to others that we sincerely care about what they have to say.

There is another level of listening that most of us never fully master. Level 3 listening is the highest level of listening. It is at this level that we are not only paying attention to what others are saying, but also what they mean and how they feel. At this level of listening, we are paying attention to gestures, facial expressions, body language, and anything else that would help us truly understand what the person is saying as well as what he or she is failing to say.

Can you imagine how your relationships will improve when you begin to really listen to others? Fred Rogers said, "Anything that's human is mentionable, and anything that is mentionable can be more manageable. When we can talk about our feelings, they become less overwhelming, less upsetting, and less scary. The people we trust with that important talk can help us know that we are not alone."

When you begin to listen well, you are modeling for others how it is done. In this way, your relationships will improve, and when that happens, your happiness and peace improve as well.

> *"Love begins with listening."*
> —FRED ROGERS

Meditation

I listen, truly listen, to others without interruption.

Action

- I will do my best to ignore distractions while I am listening to others.

- I will focus on what others are saying to me rather than how I will respond.

- I will pay attention to all aspects of someone who is speaking to me so that I can seek to understand the real meaning beneath their words.

Listening without interruption is an act of love. One of the best gifts we can give others is to listen to them. One of the most significant things we can teach to those within our influence is to model sincere listening.

On a scale of 1–10, 10 being highest, how would you rate your ability to truly listen to others? How will you increase your score?

DAY 8
BE A FRIEND

*"You can make more friends in two months
by becoming interested in other people
than you can in two years by trying to
get other people interested in you."*
—DALE CARNEGIE

B e a friend. Being a good friend comes naturally to some, but to many people, it does not. Those of us who have not experienced or witnessed healthy, authentic friendships may make mistakes that cost us friendships. In some cases, we never understand what we did wrong. When we do not learn from painful situations, we are likely to repeat our missteps.

So, let's get back to the basics of being a friend. A good friend is kind, honest, trustworthy, nurturing, humorous, and protective. They are not afraid to be themselves in front of you. They are not trying to be like you, and they are not trying to get you to become more like them. A good friend accepts you the way you are.

It may surprise you to learn that a good friend does not have to share your opinions or your values or beliefs. Some of the best friendships are between people who are very different from one another, but who allow the other person to simply be who they are. Bestselling business author, John Kador, said, "You don't have to see eye-to-eye to walk hand-in-hand. You just have to want to go in the same direction."

Good friends are helpful. They are there for you when you need them to be, and they give you space when you need that too. Good friends do not insist on certain quotas of time that must be spent with them in order to maintain the friendship.

There are ebbs and flows in good friendships. There may be times when you see each other all the time, and there may be seasons of life where you do not see each other for months. Even when we are in seasons of life where our circumstances may keep us apart, a true friendship will pick back up where we left off as though no time had passed.

We can be our authentic selves without judgment around a true friend, and the same is true for them. For example, they do not automatically end the friendship if we say the wrong thing. A real friend will consider the circumstances and the meaning behind what we have said. They know our hearts, so they give us the benefit of the doubt. They give us a pass when we are tired or ill, and they hold us accountable when we are misguided. When a real friend forgives, they do not bring it up again.

When something awesome happens for us, true friends are happy for us. They are not jealous or envious, they do not try to diminish the good thing that has happened, because they want us to be happy.

When we make the effort to be a good friend, we are showing others how to do it and are developing friendships that enrich our lives. Relationships with good friends can be one of the most meaningful aspects of this life.

"To be honest with you, I don't have the words to make you feel better, but I do have the arms to give you a hug, ears to listen to whatever you want to talk about, and I have a heart; a heart that's aching to see you smile again."
—LAURA ORTIZ

Meditation

I am a good friend, and I cherish my good friends.

Action

- I will do my best to be a good friend.

- I will tell my friends that I am grateful for them.

- I will nurture my good friendships.

In order to have good friends, we need to be a good friend. Make friendships a priority in your life, and you will enrich your life exponentially. One of the best ways to show love is to be a good friend.

On a scale of 1–10, 10 being highest, how would you rate your ability to be a friend? How will you increase your score?

DAY 9

OFFER ADVICE OR CORRECTION

"If you love someone, you will correct them or offer advice. If you do not love someone, you will not correct them or offer advice."

—ADAPTED FROM PROVERBS 13:24

Be willing offer advice or correction. It may seem counterintuitive, but it is an act of love to let someone know when they are wrong. It is an act of love because it takes time, it can be awkward, and there is always the possibility that the other person will not receive it well. When that happens, the relationship can be jeopardized. Nevertheless, when we truly care about someone, we will offer advice or correction when we think it will help the other person.

When we become aware of an area in which we can help another person improve, it is important to check our motives before giving advice or bringing correction. If your motive is purely to help the other person, that is great. Then consider your status in that person's life. If you are not in a personal or professional relationship with the other person, it is not likely that they will gratefully receive the advice you give.

Ask yourself if you are in a position to counsel, mentor, coach, or teach. If you have earned the right within the context of relationship to bring advice or correction, be sure to do it with no personal motivation. The context of your relationship will determine your approach. For example, if you are in a position of leadership, advice and correction is a natural part of the relationship. If you are on equal footing with the person as in the case of a personal friendship or a co-worker relationship, understand that by offering advice, you are opening the door to the other person giving you advice or correction. When that happens, receive it in the same way you would hope the other person would receive well-intended advice from you.

If you are not in leadership over the person, ask first if you may give the person a piece of advice. In every case, start the conversation by expressing your care and concern for the person. Say something like, "I care about you, and I want the best for you. I can see a potential problem for you, and I want to help you deal with it."

Be gentle. Be kind. Consider using the "sandwich" technique, which means to give your advice or correction between two layers of praise. For example, you might start with, "I've noticed that you are really good at being a friend. You always offer to help others. I'm concerned, though, that you are putting yourself in a position to be taken advantage of. You don't need to constantly help others in order to keep them as friends. You are awesome just the way you are!"

Another important factor in giving advice or correction is to bring correction to others in private conversations. The old saying is, "Correct in private, praise in public."

"*The true secret of giving advice is, after you have honestly given it, to be perfectly indifferent to whether it is taken or not, and never persist in trying to set people right.*"

—Henry Ward Beecher

Meditation

It is always with the best intentions that I give advice or correction.

Action

- I will always give advice or bring correction without personal motive.

- I will begin and end giving advice or correction with a compliment.

- I will give advice or correction with kindness and concern for the other person.

When we take the time and endure the awkwardness of sitting down with someone to give advice or bring correction, we show that we care enough to invest in that person and in our relationship. Only people who genuinely care will take the time to help someone do better.

On a scale of 1–10, 10 being highest, how would you rate your ability to give advice or bring correction? How will you increase your score?

DAY 10
NURTURE

"Be the one who nurtures and builds. Be the one who has an understanding and a forgiving heart, one who looks for the best in people. Leave people better than you found them."
—MARVIN J. ASHTON

Nurture people. To nurture is to look for the best in others and to help their good traits grow and develop. To nurture a person is to believe that there is good inside of them, even when you do not see it.

One of the best gifts of love that we can give or receive is to nurture ourselves and others. Nurturing the good that is within is like watering seeds and delighting as we see them grow.

Examples of ways to nurture people include recognizing the good in others, celebrating the successes of others, refusing to hold grudges against them, and spending quality time with them. Many of the other ways to love that are expounded upon in this book are actually ways to nurture others, including giving others the benefit of the doubt, believing the best of others, doing acts of service, forgiving others, and really listening with an intent to hear and understand them.

When we believe that there is good in someone, we are better able to invest the time to nurture the good in them and to nurture our relationships with them.

Nurturing others often results in the person discovering good things about themselves that they might otherwise have never recognized. You might be surprised to learn that many people grow up without ever hearing a positive word spoken about them or without ever receiving a nurturing touch. For some people, receiving a compliment, a hug or a friendly hand on their shoulder is like pouring water on parched earth. For some, your nurturing will sink in and revive a tired spirit.

Nurturing can be life-changing because when someone acknowledges a good trait within themselves of which they were previously unaware, it can be transformational. The person's self-esteem increases, which improves the person's level of confidence, which can empower them to take steps toward their good future. Someone with confidence is more likely to take calculated risks toward the fulfillment of their destiny than people who are uncertain about themselves and who don't feel an innate sense of worth and value.

Whether nurturing yourself and others is new to you or you are a natural nurturer, here are some ways that may help you improve your ability to nurture well. Decide today that you will be intentional about nurturing yourself and others. Make the effort to communicate clearly what you want and need, and listen to what those closest to you want and need. Show appreciation to those who nurture you. Take responsibility for your attitudes, words, and actions, but let's give ourselves and others a break. Even when we're not at our best, we are usually doing the best we can, given our circumstances. Provide emotional support. Share your goals and dreams. Refuse to give up on those closest to you and let them know it.

Nurturing ourselves and others can help break through old patterns and obstacles that hold us back. Start today to be good to yourself. When you do that, it will be easier to be good to others.

"We've got this gift of love, but love is like a precious plant. You can't just accept it and leave it in the cupboard or just think it's going to get on by itself. You've got to keep watering it. You've got to really look after it and nurture it."
—John Lennon

Meditation

I nurture myself and others.

Action

- I will do something good for myself today.

- I will do something good for someone else today.

- I will develop a reputation for building others up, not for tearing them down.

Nurturing may not come naturally to us, but we can develop the ability to nurture ourselves and others by adopting a mindset of building people up and leaving them better than we found them.

On a scale of 1–10, 10 being highest, how would you rate your ability to nurture? How will you increase your score?

DAY 11
KINDNESS

*"Every act of kindness is a piece
of love we leave behind."*
—PAUL WILLIAMS,
AMERICAN COMPOSER

B e kind. Kindness is a choice. It requires very little effort, no money, and a great deal of intentionality.

Some people mistake kindness with weakness, but the reality is that kindness is powerful enough to change people and circumstances in ways that we often believe to be impossible. Misunderstandings regarding the power of kindness typically originate with the thought that kindness is synonymous with being polite.

It is true that kind people are polite, but not all polite people are authentically kind. In the same way, acts of kindness do not guarantee that a person is honest and has integrity. It has been said that even the infamous organized crime boss, Al Capone, to whom countless murders and other crimes have been attributed, was courteous and polite.

Authentic kindness is a virtuous character trait that has no motive other than to value others. Real kindness expects nothing in return; an act of authentic kindness is its own reward. This kindness trait informs and influences everything that the truly kind person thinks and does. Authentic kindness becomes part of your identity, influences your attitudes and informs your behaviors. For example, a genuinely kind person refuses to take offense when an insult is lobbed their way. Rather than return insult for insult, the kind person responds in a kind way. Instead of assuming that the offensive person means to harm them, they assume that there is something wrong in that person's life that drives them to behave the way they do. A kind person chooses empathy over judgment. It isn't hard to imagine, then, that people who are truly kind are able to maintain their peace and happiness simply because they don't easily get hurt or let themselves grow angry by taking offense.

Being an authentically kind person is often an indicator of a healthy level of self-esteem. It is easier for truly kind people to respond with kindness to just about anything that comes their way because they are confident in their worth and value. They know that no one can diminish them, so they are not defensive, nor are they offensive.

It is important that we not reserve our acts of kindness only for those who deserve them. Let's not wait to be kind to only those who are kind to us. By leading the way in kindness, we are modeling kind behavior for others.

Acts of kindness can have the power to uplift people from sadness, depression, and even despair. They can release tension, de-escalate arguments, and help to repair damaged relationships. This is especially true when given to people who are unable to reciprocate, such as people who are ill, grieving, or who are suffering. Examples of genuine acts of kindness are including people who are often overlooked, making people feel welcomed and included, and making those who are frightened feel safer in our presence.

Authentically kind people give dignity to others by making eye contact, listening well, smiling genuinely at others, and expecting nothing in return. In so doing, they influence others through their lifestyle of kindness.

"Unexpected kindness is the most powerful, least costly, and most underrated agent of human change."
—BOB KERREY,
FORMER NEBRASKA GOVERNOR

Meditation

I am a genuinely kind person.

Action

- I will practice an act of kindness today and expect nothing in return.

- I will think of myself as an authentically kind person.

- I will be kind to myself today.

Kindness is a beautiful way to show love to others, especially when it is unconditional, offered freely, and given to anyone regardless of their socio-economic status, skin color, gender, religious preference, political affiliation, or any of the other ways in which we divide and label ourselves and others.

On a scale of 1–10, 10 being highest, how would you rate your ability to nurture? How will you increase your score?

DAY 12
ENCOURAGE

"A word of encouragement during
a failure is worth more than an
hour of praise after success."

—Anonymous

ncourage yourself and others. To encourage someone is to give them words or actions that provide inspiration, support, confidence, or hope. Everyone needs encouragement now and then, and almost everyone appreciates a genuine word of encouragement. However, for someone who has not received a great deal of it, it can make a dramatic difference.

The people who can benefit most from your encouragement are those who are struggling or suffering with something that you have successfully overcome. For example, if a person is trying to lose weight, someone who has successfully lost weight and kept it off can provide encouragement that is far more meaningful than someone who has been slender their whole life and has never known the feeling of facing the difficult challenge of weight loss.

When we encourage someone, we are literally telling them that we believe in them and in their ability to overcome the obstacle that is standing in their way or successfully survive the challenge that they're facing. Encouragement, especially from someone we respect, can be the motivation we need to get us over the finish line.

One of the best ways to encourage others is to acknowledge their struggle or suffering. Sometimes it helps to just know that someone has noticed that you are in a tough place.

Another way to encourage others is to praise their efforts and progress regardless of how small. People tend to do more of what they get positive attention for, so give praise liberally. The caveat to that is to not give empty praise. No one wants to hear, "You're doing great" when it is obvious that you are not. By the same token, let's never be dismissive about the struggles of others by saying things like, "It'll be fine," or, "Don't worry, you'll be great" if we aren't confident that it really will work out.

We can encourage people in their abilities and in their innate worth. We can value others by reminding them of their good personality or character traits or by noticing their virtuous behavior, such as ways they have helped us or how we have seen them help others. Knowing that we have had a positive impact on others makes us feel better. A reminder of our contribution to others or to the greater good is a powerful morale booster.

One powerful way to encourage others is to say a few words about a person's character, strength, or talents when we introduce them. Everyone stands up a little taller when someone publicly mentions something good about them. For example, "I want you to meet my son-in-law, who is one of the most encouraging people I've ever known."

"Too often we underestimate the power of a touch, a smile, a kind word, a listening ear, an honest compliment, or the smallest act of caring, all of which have the potential to turn a life around."

—LEO BUSCAGLIA

Meditation

I am a positive encourager.

Action

- I will encourage myself every day in everything.

- I will seek out someone to encourage.

- I will encourage others with every opportunity that presents itself.

Encouragement can be as simple as sending a text or a written note that says, "I'm here for you," "I'm thinking of you," or "I'm praying for you." It can be the power of your presence in a phone call or a visit or sending flowers or a small gift. However, you do it, do it and two people will feel better.

On a scale of 1–10, 10 being highest, how would you rate your ability to encourage? How will you increase your score?

DAY 13
COMPLIMENT

"I will be generous with my love today. I will sprinkle compliments and uplifting words everywhere I go. I will do this knowing that my words are like seeds and when they fall on fertile soil, a reflection of those seeds will grow into something greater."

—STEVE MARABOLI

C ompliment others. When we recognize people, we give them dignity. When we compliment them, we are virtually saying, "I see you. I hear you. I value you."

When we identify the goodness inside of people, it makes them feel better. You might be surprised to learn that for some people, no one has ever taken the time to compliment their skills, talents, abilities, character traits, intelligence, or personality.

When we get the opportunity to identify a skill, talent, or character or personality trait within someone for the first time, we have the exciting opportunity to give dignity to that person, and possibly to even spark transformation in that person.

When we compliment a person about a specific thing that is good about them, it is as though we are holding up a mirror for that person and allowing him or her to see the worth and value that is within. This one quick, simple, free act gives dignity, builds self-esteem, and increases the person's confidence. A specific, authentic compliment is empowering.

Although compliments about personality and abilities are great, and compliments about a person's appearance are courteous, the most empowering compliments are about good character traits. If we want to truly build a person up, complimenting their character is the best way to do that. For example, noticing that someone is exceptionally resilient, resourceful, courageous, brave, or perseverant is far more meaningful than complimenting someone's hair style or some other aspect of their physical appearance.

It's a statement about the superficial nature of our culture that many of the compliments people tend to give others are about physical appearance, something they own or something they've done. If you think about it, we typically compliment others on what they are wearing, their hair, their new car, or their new home. We may compliment them on an achievement by their child or how well trained their dog is, but when was the last time you heard anyone compliment the good character trait of another? We will talk more about this tomorrow.

Of course, there is nothing wrong with complimenting physical appearance, etc., but it is the compliments about the ways we excel, the things that we do well, the things that we are most passionate about doing, our talents, and who we are truly are on the inside, that are most meaningful.

Almost everyone enjoys talking about the things that they are passionate about. So, a compliment about the thing that we enjoy doing above all else is a conversation starter and could be a relationship starter.

"Compliment people. Magnify their strengths, not their weaknesses."

—JOYCE MEYER

Meditation

I look for the good in people, and I compliment them on it.

Action

- I will notice the good in someone, and I will point it out to them today.

- I will compliment someone today.

- I will consider my own good character traits and give myself credit for them.

Compliments tell people of their worth and value. They affirm and empower them. You have the power to do that for everyone within your influence. Every time you give someone a specific, genuine compliment, you are giving love. If you will do this consistently, it will become a habit, and when this habit becomes a lifestyle, you will find that love is consistently splashing back up on you.

On a scale of 1–10, 10 being highest, how would you rate your ability to give authentic compliments? How will you increase your score?

DAY 14

RECOGNIZE GOOD CHARACTER

"Character is not something that you buy; it is not a commodity that can be bartered for; it is not a quality suited for only the rich and famous; rather, character is built upon the foundational commitment of love, honesty, and compassion for others."

—BYRON R. PULSIFER

Recognizing good character often results in people exercising more of those character traits. Character is the essence of a person, so when we point out a person's good character traits, we are literally telling them (or reminding them) who they really are.

Pointing out the good character traits of a person is important, but it is exceptionally powerful with young people, with people who have made poor decisions, and with people who have been put down or who have been verbally or physically abused.

It has been said that we become like the people with whom we spend the most time. If the people we are with are of good character, that is great. If not, the time we are spending with people of poor character can literally change the trajectory of our lives for the worse.

Given the level of unfiltered violence and graphic content available 24/7, we are exposed to thoughts, words, and images that are influencing us in ways that we may not even be aware of. We are being influenced by television, movies, social media, videos, and music that are normalizing attitudes, thoughts, and behaviors that our good character traits may never have previously accepted as appropriate. Character eroding influences have crept into our culture.

Some of these changes have been abrupt and others have happened gradually and more subtly. Either way, it is up to us to take inventory of our good character traits and to be diligent about maintaining them.

People of good character are the role models that others look up to regardless of what they see in other places. Good character is timeless. It does not shift with the trends or adapt to the culture. People of good character are the pillars of our families and our communities. These are the role models we should find and emulate for the next generation.

Some good character traits to intentionally develop are honesty, integrity, resilience, perseverance, determination, optimism, bravery, responsiveness, adaptability, tenacity, and conscientiousness. For a more in-depth consideration of good character traits, search the internet and spend some time learning about what you find. When you do, you will find some character traits that resonate with you. You will find yourself there, and when you do, you will have made a powerful discovery.

"The right way is not always the popular and easy way. Standing for right when it is unpopular is a true test of moral character."

—Margaret Chase Smith

Meditation

I am a person of good character.

Action

- I will identify my good character traits.

- I will exercise the character traits that I want to embody.

- I will notice and point out the good character traits of others.

Since the essence of who we are as unique-in-all-the-world individuals are our character traits, let's identify them, learn about them, and exercise them like we would exercise our muscles. What we focus on will grow to the point that we become influencers for good.

On a scale of 1–10, 10 being highest, how would you rate your good character traits? How will you increase your score?

DAY 15
FORGIVE

"When you hold resentment toward another, you are bound to that person or condition by an emotional link that is stronger than steel. Forgiveness is the only way to dissolve that link and get free."

—CATHERINE PONDER

F orgiving is intentional and is one of the most powerful things we can do for ourselves. It is our prerogative to forgive another (or not), and it is completely within our control. It may be one of the most difficult things we ever do, but for our own health and wellbeing, it must be done.

True forgiveness must be voluntary and intentional to result in a change in feeling and attitude about an offense or victimization. The most important thing to know about forgiveness is that the person who has done wrong does not need to deserve it or even to ask for it in order for us to give it. The hard truth is that forgiveness is always undeserved.

It has been said that holding tightly to the anger and bitterness that results after being hurt is like eating poison and hoping the offender will suffer and die. Any logic in this is clearly flawed. It is the holder of the anger who suffers. It is actually far more rewarding to forgive and move on to live a happy, peaceful life. It may be worse for the offender when you do so. As poet and playwright, Oscar Wilde, said, "Always forgive your enemies— nothing annoys them so much."

Some studies suggest that forgiving someone who has hurt us produces significant measurable benefits for the one who forgives. Some of the benefits can include alleviation of depression, anxiety, anger, and even post-traumatic stress symptoms.

Most people cannot simply make up their mind one day to forgive and completely forget. Before you begin the process of forgiveness, acknowledge the wrong, rather than ignoring it.

Do not try to pretend it did not happen. That is not forgiveness, so the pain of the offense will only show up in your life at another time. As Dr. Bessel Van Der Kolk has said, "The body keeps the score, brain, mind, and body."

Some suggestions for how to forgive include, giving the offender the benefit of the doubt, at least until there is no doubt. Consider that the person may have done the best he or she could do given what they knew at the time. Consider that the person who harmed you may not be in his or her right mind. Mental, physical, and emotional factors can cause people to behave in ways that are inappropriate and out of character for them.

All of this consideration for the person who harmed you is not to make excuses for them, but rather to develop empathy. One of the greatest tools for forgiveness is to develop empathy for the people who harm us. It can be powerful to imagine that person as a small, vulnerable child. Consider what may have happened in that person's life to result in their ability to harm another. Consider also that something may be seriously wrong with

87

the person. We never really know what other people are going through or dealing with.

Finally, one of the most powerful tools to lead to our ability to forgive is to find meaning in our painful experiences. If we are able to see the lessons from what we have been through and see that we're stronger, more resilient, and more capable because of the painful experience, we are better able to forgive the person who caused the pain. When we have truly mastered this ability, we may even thank the person for causing the pain that ultimately resulted in us being better for the experience.

> *"Forgiveness is unlocking the door to set someone free and realizing you were the prisoner!"*
> —MAX LUCADO

Meditation

I am quick to forgive others.

Action

- I refuse to hold on to offense.

- I will take inventory of any grudges I am holding onto, and I will forgive those who have caused me pain.

- I will forgive myself for any guilt I am holding onto.

Learning to forgive ourselves and others is difficult, but when we begin the work of forgiveness, it gets easier and easier. Before long, it becomes part of who we are, as evidenced by our character trait of mercy. Merciful people are loving people. The more quickly we show mercy, the more love we will feel.

On a scale of 1–10, 10 being highest, how would you rate your ability to forgive? How will you increase your score?

DAY 16

GIVE THE BENEFIT OF THE DOUBT

*"I will be merciful, and I will believe in people.
If I am to err, I will err on the side of mercy.
I will give people the benefit of the doubt.
I will bend, but not break, in order to give
people the opportunity to grow and develop."*
—DAVID K. BERNARD

Give the benefit of the doubt. For a relationship to be good, we must have an element of trust. To give the benefit of the doubt, there must first be trust. Trust is the foundation on which all good relationships are built. Without trust, the relationship is superficial at best.

Consider how you feel about trust. In doing so, it might be easier to think about the opposite of trust, which can be characterized by suspicions, deceit, and betrayal. We humans tend to hate it when someone lies to us or betrays us in some way. So, while the thought of trust may not be on the top of our mind, it is significant to us.

Our ability to trust someone determines the degree to which we are able to give that person the benefit of the doubt. If we trust someone implicitly, we automatically give them the benefit of the doubt. In fact, we have no doubt about what that person could do wrong (or could never do). As a result, we are quick to defend the person. As an example, think of the best person you know. Now think about what you would say if someone told you that the best person you know had just robbed a bank. You would think that it was absurd, and you would automatically jump to that person's defense. There is no way that the best person you know would ever rob a bank.

Now think about someone you know who you do not trust. Perhaps this is someone who has made some poor choices. Maybe this is someone who has been in trouble with the law in the past. If someone were to tell you that this person just robbed a bank, you might not automatically jump to their defense. You might have a little more trouble giving them the benefit of the doubt.

Of course, we would like to be able to trust everyone in our lives. We would like to only have the kinds of relationships where we have implicit trust in others. However, the reality of relationships is that they can be messy. It takes time in the context of relationships to develop trust in others and for them to trust us. Our levels of trust vary from person to person and relationship to relationship, but regardless of how we feel about a person, the loving thing to do is always to give others the benefit of the doubt, at least until there is no doubt.

To give someone the benefit of the doubt is to believe the best about them regardless of what others say or what the evidence may point to before all the facts are available. It means to give people an opportunity to tell their side of the story. It means never jumping to conclusions. It is really listening with the intent to hear and understand before drawing a conclusion. In its truest form, it involves accepting the person's version of the story as true even though we do not have evidence to prove its veracity.

Ultimately, giving someone the benefit of the doubt is a choice. If we want to have love in our lives, the loving choices must be made.

"Love chooses to believe the best about people. It gives them the benefit of the doubt. It refuses to fill in the unknowns with negative assumptions. And when our worst hopes are proven to be true, love makes every effort to deal with them and move forward. As much as possible, love focuses on the positive."
—Stephen Kendrick

Meditation

I give the benefit of the doubt.

Action

- I will defend people who are accused without all the facts.

- I will listen with the intent to hear and understand before making a judgment.

- I will always believe the best of people until I have definitive proof that they really are guilty of wrongdoing.

Believing the best of people will earn you a reputation for being a fair and just person. When we have that reputation, people will believe the best of us and be more likely to forgive us when we misstep.

On a scale of 1–10, 10 being highest, how would you rate your ability to give the benefit of the doubt? How will you increase your score?

DAY 17

EMPOWER OTHERS

"When you believe in someone you profoundly increase their ability to have faith in themselves and achieve. When you love someone you imprint on their heart something so powerful that it changes the trajectory of their life. When you do both, you set into motion, a gift to the world…because those who are believed in and loved understand the beauty of a legacy and the absolute duty of paying it forward."

—Jason Versey

Empowering others means, literally, to give them our power or to put power in them. To empower someone is to help build their confidence, to enable and equip them to find and fulfill their purpose and destiny. To lend or to give someone power helps build their energy, inspiration, and enthusiasm. Second only to giving love, empowering someone is the best thing that we can do for another person.

To lend power to someone means to defend them to others, to stand up for them against a bully or a group that is detracting from or disempowering them. To stand up for someone is to give them a voice, to give them individual or group agency, which means to give them the power to speak up and to act on their behalf where they previously did not have the freedom to do so.

To give someone power means more than just advocacy—it means to give them what they need to stand up for themselves. Some examples of empowerment include educating someone on things such as coping skills, communication techniques, or life skills; providing them with things they need, such as a place to live or transportation to and from work.

In the workplace, empowering someone can include giving them a say in the way things are done or giving authority about something, as in the case of an employer giving an employee the authority to resolve an issue for a dissatisfied customer or having a say about policies or procedures.

Every one of us can empower others by lending them our power. We can speak up when someone is speaking disparagingly about someone we know. We can speak up when we see injustice. For example, we can write letters to editors to stand up for people or groups of people who don't have the power to speak up for themselves.

We all have the ability to empower others, but those of us in leadership positions have the authority and responsibility to give power to others to help them learn and grow in order to help them achieve their potential. One example of this is parents and guardians who can give children and teens chores and projects that teach them skills, responsibility, and work ethic.

Those of us who supervise others at work can give power to employees by teaching what we know, sharing information, listening to their suggestions, and by recognizing their successes as well as the times that they tried to do something and failed. If we give people credit for trying, they are far more likely to try again. Conversely, if we ignore their attempts, or worse, chide them for their failure, they will likely withdraw and not try again. Bosses who empower their employees help them develop their skills which improves efficiency and profitability in the workplace.

We can also give power to others by being willing to give a reference or recommendation, by vouching for their good character, or being willing to introduce them to our friends. Many of us have opportunities to listen to the ideas of others, teach what we know, and share the wisdom we have acquired. Sadly, some people do not teach and share with others. Some hold back because they do not think it is their role, or they do not think they have anything of value to offer, or in some cases they hold back because they are threatened by the other person. Some people think that if they share what they know, the other person will get ahead, and they will be left behind.

Even when we are in a highly competitive environment, giving love by empowering others is the choice that helps us rise above the noise and distractions of this life. When we do the right thing, ultimately, the right things will happen for us.

> *"The ultimate use of power is to empower others."*
> —WILLIAM GLASSER

Meditation

I empower myself and others.

Action

- I will lend my power to others by defending those who are being mistreated.

- I will give power to others by mentoring, coaching, or teaching them what I know.

- I will empower myself by believing in myself and in my ability to empower others.

Using our personal power to empower others who have no voice or who are not as powerful or confident as we are, is some of the best and highest use of our power.

On a scale of 1–10, 10 being highest, how would you rate your ability to empower others? How will you increase your score?

DAY 18

CHOOSE THE RIGHT TIMING

"Ask any comedian, tennis player, or chef. Timing is everything."
—MEG ROSOFF

Choose the right timing in love, relationships, work, and life. Can you imagine asking someone to marry you while they are in their annual review meeting with their boss? You would never pose one of the most important questions of your life to a person who is not able to pay attention to you. To choose the wrong timing could be disastrous.

If we value relationships, we will choose the right timing for every important conversation. To have a serious conversation about our feelings or the future of our relationships, we need to choose a time and a place where we will have privacy, a place that is quiet enough to really hear the person, and a place where we will not be rushed. We will choose a time when the other person is not doing something that would distract them from looking at us and listening to us. We will choose a time other than when the person has just awakened, just walked in from a long day at work, is in the middle of a task, or is on a deadline.

It is not difficult to see that choosing the wrong timing to talk about something that is important to us could lead to disappointment, disillusionment, or anger.

Timing is also important in our work, studies, and in every area of our life. If we do not give appropriate, ample time to something that we care about, we will not do our best. If we want to live a life of love and happiness and joy, we will make good use of the 1,440 minutes we get every day of our lives. When we do not choose the right timing, we can squander precious time of our lives—time that we can never get back.

The wealthiest person in the world and the poorest person in the world each gets the exact same amount of time. The same is true for the most popular people and the least known people. The happiest and the saddest, and so on. The time of our lives is the truest measure of our lives because it represents what is possible. Time can be invested into our potential or wasted in ways that do not enhance our lives, or worse, that diminish or even destroy our lives.

Time is ours to use to develop what we want in this life. Love is obviously important to you because you are reading this book. So, by reading this book and implementing its 30 suggestions, you are investing time in developing love—good for you!

So, the question becomes how to choose the right timing. The first consideration is to think about what the perfect circumstances would be for the conversation, activity, or goal that you want to happen. Then work backwards to make plans that, if executed well, should culminate in the results you want to achieve.

If another person is involved, consider how you would feel about the time, place, and other circumstances involved in your plan. For example, if you want to ask your boss for a raise, consider the boss' obligations, including other meetings, project deadlines, etc., and ask yourself if what you have planned would work well if you were the boss. If the answer is no, then revise your plans. The same goes for all other important conversations. Begin with what you would like to achieve, and then envision the perfect timing and circumstances it will take to make it happen.

"Timing is everything. Tell me how a young man spends his evenings and I will tell you how far he is likely to go in the world. The popular notion is that a youth's progress depends upon how he acts during his working hours. It doesn't. It depends far more upon how he utilizes his leisure...If he spends it in harmless idleness, he is likely to be kept on the payroll, but that will be about all. If he diligently utilizes his own time...to fit himself for more responsible duties, then

the greater responsibilities—and greater rewards—are almost certain to come to him."
—B.C. Forbes

Meditation

I give careful consideration to timing.

Action

- I will plan important events to accomplish my desired goals.

- I will honor the time of others by choosing the right time for important conversations.

- I will invest the 1,440 minutes I get every day to achieve my goal of having more love in my life.

Investing your time well and choosing the right timing for the important things in your life will reap great results for you. It will earn you respect from others who value their time. And it will model the value of the preciousness of time for everyone within your influence.

On a scale of 1–10, 10 being highest, how would you rate your ability to choose the right timing? How will you increase your score?

DAY 19

REFUSE TO GET HURT OR OFFENDED

"Weak people revenge. Strong people forgive. Intelligent people ignore."
—ALBERT EINSTEIN

Refuse to take offense at anything that is said or done to you, even if it is meant as a painful insult or slight.

Many people miss the fact that taking offense at an intentional insult or slight is actually giving the offender precisely what he or she wants. Never give offenders the satisfaction of letting them get to you. If they do get to you, do not give them the pleasure of knowing it. Never let them see you cry.

Most of the things that hurt or offend us are not intentionally done to harm us. The typical things at which people take offense happen when people are so busy or focused on their own issues that they forget us or unintentionally do something that hurts us.

Remember that there is a distinct difference between the words "hurt" and "harm". To hurt someone is to cause injury. To harm someone is to intentionally cause injury. Most of the hurts in our lives have been unintentionally caused. Family members or friends who forget to send a birthday card, call when we are ill, or invite us to their party probably are not intentionally trying to harm us, but the feeling of having been forgotten or left out can sting.

Even in the case of betrayal, the offender usually does not wake up in the morning with the intent to harm their loved one, for example, but they allow themselves to be in places and in circumstances where the predictable thing happens, and they find themselves cheating. They often compound the problem by lying to try to protect the person they care about. Their actions (or failure to act, as in the case of failure to leave before it is too late), causes great hurt.

The pain that we feel when we are hurt unintentionally by people who care about us is rooted in the fact that we have given our worth and value over to others. Even the most self-confident people will feel pain when they are betrayed, but for the person who is confident in his or her value as a unique and priceless person, the pain won't be as deep, and it will not last as long as it will for a person who needs the approval of others to confirm their worth and value.

Value yourself as the awesome person you are. When we are confident in our inherent value, regardless of what others think of us, we can simply refuse to take offense.

"Good sense makes one slow to anger, and it is his glory to overlook an offense."
—PROVERBS 19:11

Meditation

I know my value and I refuse to be harmed by others.

Action

- I will ignore the insults or slights of others.

- I will forgive people who hurt me whether intentional or unintentional.

- I will not allow anger to steal precious time away from me.

As we rise higher in refusing to take offense, let's remember that there are times when we, too, will unintentionally hurt someone. We will forget an important date, fail to make a call, or leave someone out. When we adopt a lifestyle of ignoring offenses, we are modeling this for others. Hopefully, they will rise up too and extend us the courtesy of ignoring our faults and failings.

On a scale of 1–10, 10 being highest, how would you rate your ability to ignore insults or slights? How will you increase your score?

DAY 20
HELP OTHERS IN NEED

"The purpose of life is not to be happy. It is to be useful, to be honorable, to be compassionate, to have it make some difference that you have lived and lived well."
—RALPH WALDO EMERSON

Helping others in need is noble and honorable. It is a good thing to do and can be tremendously rewarding...but let's be honest, it can also be extremely difficult.

Some people who are in need do not think they need help. Some who are in need refuse help from others. Other people receive help, yet no matter how much they receive, they want more. Helping others in need does not always lead to warm and fuzzy feelings for everyone concerned. Nevertheless, it's important that we learn the best ways to approach helping others who are in need, and do what we can to help regardless of how it's received.

Before we help people who are in need, we need to first understand what they think they need and want. We can do more damage than good when we "parachute" into the lives of others with a predetermined prescription that we think will "fix" what we think is broken in their lives. When we make assumptions about what is needed without first taking the time to hear from the people who are in need, we can spend a lot of energy, time, and money doing something that doesn't need to be done or something that is well-intended but ultimately misguided. These good intentions and priceless resources are wasted.

The best way to determine how to best help others is to first look them in the eyes and ask them what they need. Engage the people who need help in the process without assuming that you know what's best.

The act of asking and then listening intently, without interruption, gives dignity and agency to the person in need. It acknowledges that the person is the world's foremost expert on his or her life, and that the person knows their circumstances, surroundings, and resources better than you do. To do otherwise is to diminish the other person.

Of course, if the person in need is not in the mental or physical condition to be able to have a meaningful conversation or to make an accurate assessment of their circumstances, then, by all means, do your best to meet the needs that you see and that you are able to meet, or reach out to some government agency, non-profit organization, or individual who is able to appropriately assist.

Robert Woodson, founder of the Woodson Center and author of Lessons From The Least of These, has seen evidence over decades of successfully helping people in impoverished communities that people can be the agents of their own uplift when engaged directly and assisted with the resources to do so. Woodson says that the key to success in helping others is to empower them to help themselves. To do that, he says, "Relationships are the necessary condition for transforming others, and trust is the common currency."

One of the best ways that we can help others who are in need is to be a friend, to take the time to really listen, and to be willing to do what we can to help them help themselves.

"No one is useless in this world who lightens the burdens of another."
—CHARLES DICKENS

Meditation

I seek to help others without assuming I have all the answers.

Action

- I will ask someone in need how I might be of service.

- I will listen to people in need to learn what they need and want.

- I will never assume that I know best what someone else needs.

As we become aware of people in need, we may also become more aware of our own needs and wants. In adopting a mindset of helping others to help themselves, we may find new ways to help ourselves.

On a scale of 1–10, 10 being highest, how would you rate your ability to help others in need? How will you increase your score?

GIVE OPPORTUNITIES

"If somebody offers you an amazing opportunity but you are not sure you can do it, say yes—then learn how to do it later."

—RICHARD BRANSON

Give opportunities. One of the most powerful gifts we can give someone is an opportunity to learn something, to do something or to be included in something for which they might not otherwise be welcome.

When we give opportunities to others, we are saying that we believe in them and in their ability to do well. To give someone an opportunity is to cheer them on. There is nothing more rewarding than to have a ringside seat in the life of someone who seizes an opportunity and makes the most of it. To watch someone use their skills, talents, and abilities to help others in their own unique way is to empower them to succeed. Giving opportunity is the catalyst for empowerment, and empowerment is the doorway to fulfilling one's purpose in life.

We have all had the feeling at one time or another in our lives that all we needed was a chance, and we would show the world what we are capable of doing. We do not all get the opportunities we want, but we have all been given opportunities of one form or another.

Almost all of us can give opportunities to others. To give opportunity means to facilitate, assist, permit, enable, give the means to do something, or make it possible for the person to do something. We do not have to be an employer in order to give someone an opportunity, although giving someone a job is a great way to give a person an opportunity.

There is a type of opportunity that any one of us can provide. We give people an opportunity when we let them into our lives. When we befriend someone, we are, in effect, bringing that person into our life. When we do that, we give that person an opportunity to feel friendship, care, concern, and love. Giving someone an opportunity to enter our lives can be among the most meaningful gifts we can give.

Another easy way that each of us can give opportunities to others is to introduce someone to our friends. When we connect people, we are giving them an opportunity to make new friendships that can enrich their lives. Another is when we do something like vouching for someone's character as in the case of giving a reference for someone or recommending someone for a job. When we do that, we may be giving that person an opportunity to create a successful life and possibly even launch a successful career.

Imagine what you would like to do if you had the opportunity to do so. Some people say things like, "I'd like to meet so-and-so if only I had the occasion to do so." Or, "If I could find the right teacher, I would learn to play the piano." Or, "I would go to college if I could get a scholarship." Or, "I would go skydiving if only I had the chance."

You may not be able to make it possible for someone to go to college or learn to play the piano, but there just may be an opportunity that you, or someone you know, can easily provide that could be a once-in-a-lifetime experience for the people involved.

People who receive a meaningful opportunity are usually grateful and never forget who gave it to them. These are the people who do all they can to return the favor and to pay it forward. Whether the opportunity is significant or seemingly inconsequential, give opportunities to others whenever you can.

> *"There is no greater gift of love than to give someone an opportunity to fulfill his or her life purpose."*
> —RHONDA SCIORTINO

Meditation

I give opportunities to others.

Action

- I will look for ways to give opportunities to others.

- I will give an opportunity without expecting anything in return.

- I will show gratitude to those who have given me opportunities.

To give someone an opportunity can be transformational for the person who receives the opportunity, but also for everyone that person impacts. Families, neighborhoods, and entire communities can change when the person who receives an opportunity steps up, works hard, and makes the most of the opportunity provided.

On a scale of 1–10, 10 being highest, how would you rate your ability to give opportunities to others? How will you increase your score?

SHARE WHAT YOU HAVE

"Love only grows by sharing. You can only have more for yourself by giving it away to others."
—BRIAN TRACY

Share what you have. For some, sharing what they have comes easily. For others, especially those who have had little, sharing can be more difficult. Regardless of our financial status, there are things that all of us can easily share.

We can share a smile, a joke, a good attitude, a word of encouragement, and so much more. We can share the wisdom that we have acquired throughout our lives. For the many people who do not have a reliable person they can go to for advice, sharing our wisdom can provide the mentorship that makes an enormous difference to someone else.

Everyone does not know what you know, so everyone can benefit from your knowledge, talents, and abilities. For everything you do naturally, there is someone for whom that knowledge is a mystery. For everything you have learned how to do, there is someone who has trouble figuring it out.

In a practical sense, cleaning out our closets, garages, and kitchen cabinets and giving away things that we rarely use can make life better for others. Consider that the outfit you have not worn in over a year could be the proper attire for a job interview that could change someone's life. Your old pots and pans, dishes and utensils that have not been used in years could stock the kitchen of a teenager who is transitioning out of foster care to life on his or her own without money, family, or support. Whatever you have that you no longer need could be someone else's treasure.

Being generous makes us more attractive! When we are generous, we smile more, we feel better, and we literally attract other generous people into our lives, but how do we become more generous?

Generosity is born out of a sense of gratitude. When we are genuinely grateful for what we have, regardless of how much or how little we have, we are far more likely to share what we have. W. Clement Stone said, "If you're really thankful, what do you do? You share!"

Generosity can emanate from a sense of faith, faith in God and His goodness, faith that we will be okay, faith that we will always have what we need, and faith that everything will work out. People of faith tend to share because it is a natural outflow of the blessings they have received. They also tend to share their faith, not for the sake of proselytizing, but because they want others to feel the same sense of love and gratitude that they feel. Believing that everything will somehow work out helps to relieve suffering, and generous people are typically compassionate people who want to relieve the suffering of others.

"Maya Angelou lived what she wrote. She understood that sharing her truth connected her to the greater human truths - of longing,

abandonment, security, hope, wonder, prejudice, mystery, and, finally, self-discovery: the realization of who you really are and the liberation that love brings."

—OPRAH WINFREY

Meditation

I share what I have.

Action

- I will look for opportunities to share my knowledge and wisdom.

- I will give to others the things that I no longer regularly use.

- I will begin today to live a lifestyle of generosity.

When we adopt a generous and giving spirit towards others, it opens the door for us to share whatever we have that can benefit others. Think about the people who took an interest in you and taught you something. You can pay it forward by taking someone under your wing and teaching them what you know.

On a scale of 1–10, 10 being highest, how would you rate your ability to share with others? How will you increase your score?

INCLUDE AND WELCOME SOMEONE

"You can do what I cannot do. I can do what you cannot do. Together we can do great things."

—SAINT TERESA OF CALCUTTA

I nclude and welcome someone. We all want to feel that we are included, accepted, and that we belong. Ask anyone who has ever felt excluded and unwanted, and they will tell you that it is a terrible feeling.

To be invited, included, and welcomed is life affirming. To take it a step further, to truly embrace someone can begin to heal old wounds.

The beautiful thing about including someone is that it takes little time and no money. It is simple, and it usually does not require a great deal of effort.

When we take the step of formally including someone in our lives forever, as in the case of marrying or adopting someone, we open our hearts and our home to that person. We are literally saying, "You're one of us now. You belong here. You are a part of us, a part of a group that is bigger than all of us."

Including someone can be incredibly restorative because in addition to healing old wounds, inclusion makes it more difficult for others to harm you. Anyone who would intend to harm you has to go through others to get to you, and if, as a part of a whole group, you are hurt, healing comes easier because you are not alone.

When we are included, the bonds of relationship give us dignity, respect, and confidence. They may also give us greater access to opportunities, knowledge, and resources. Conversely, being alone closes us off from the many relationships that can result in those things.

Inclusion can increase a person's positive self-image and respect for others. It helps us learn important things from others, like problem solving techniques, conflict resolution, and other relationship skills. It helps to develop a sense of community for everyone involved. Importantly, inclusion helps us to see that where we are weak, others are strong, and vice versa. When we interact with those who have included and welcomed us, we learn to respect ourselves and others.

To include and welcome people, begin with eye contact, a smile, and welcoming words. Ask for the person's opinion. Inquire about their likes and dislikes. Invite them to participate in whatever you are doing. Practice hospitality, to make them feel comfortable in your presence.

Do what you can to help other people feel important. Show empathy when others are down by listening with the intent to hear and understand, putting yourself in the other person's place, and make an effort to spend time together to build the bonds of friendship.

"It's when we care for each other—choosing inclusion and love over division and hatred—that this great country is at its greatest."
—TULSI GABBARD

Meditation

I include and welcome others.

Action

- I will practice hospitality and make others feel welcome.

- I will help others thrive by doing what I can to make them feel important.

- I will invest time with others to build stronger friendships.

When we understand that part of a successful life is good relationships, it is easier to invest the time in creating and building strong connections with others. Creating connections with people who are different than we are enriches our lives.

On a scale of 1–10, 10 being highest, how would you rate your ability to include and welcome others? How will you increase your score?

SMILE AT SOMEONE

"What sunshine is to flowers, smiles are to humanity. These are but trifles, to be sure; but scattered along life's pathway, the good they do is inconceivable."

—JOSEPH ADDISON

S mile! A genuine smile can do so much more than we know. We rarely know what others are really going through. The neighbor we smile at and wave to as they are driving by might be headed to the hospital to see a loved one who is suffering. The person we pass in the grocery store might have just received a life-threatening medical diagnosis. The person on the other end of the customer service line might have just learned that her child is using drugs. While a smile itself cannot fix any of those things, it does confer meaning that says, "You're not alone. There is still good in the world. Please don't give up."

Smiling releases endorphins, serotonin, and other chemicals that make us feel good. It has been suggested that these chemicals have the ability to lift our spirits, relax us, reduce physical pain, lower blood pressure, boost our immune system, and possibly even extend our lives. As if that were not enough, a smile can set in motion the release of neuropeptides that can improve our neural communication, so we are actually sharper when we decide to intentionally live a life filled with smiles.

Smiling instantly improves our appearance at no cost whatsoever. Everyone looks better when they smile. Smiling makes us more approachable. People are more likely to strike up a conversation with us when we are smiling. Think about it, a genuine smile is a universally recognized expression of friendliness. It transcends all language barriers.

When every muscle in our face is engaged in a smile, our eyes crinkle up, the corners of our lips turn up, the apples of our cheeks are more pronounced, and we become more human, approachable, more likable, and more influential to those around us. How do we become more influential? Smiling! Because smiling is contagious.

A person with a genuine, full-faced smile will almost always trigger a smile in others. Our brains automatically notice facial expressions, and often, we automatically mimic the expressions of others without giving any thought to it. This is important because someone who may not feel that he or she has a reason to smile may be "triggered" to smile just by seeing your smile. Given the benefits of smiling, just transferring your smile to the face of another can literally help to lift that person's spirits.

Today's discussion would not be complete without adding that there are many different types of smiles, and there are times when the wrong smile at the wrong time can convey the wrong message. For example, a big, happy smile at a funeral is probably inappropriate. One corner of a mouth upturned into a smile that is accompanied by a sideways glance can be interpreted as a social snub. Narrowed eyes with a slight smile may be interpreted as being a sexual advance. Most people instinctively know the difference, but if you are not sure that you do, look in the mirror or ask a friend to help you intentionally create the smiles that convey the good messages that you want to communicate.

"A warm smile is the universal language of kindness."
—WILLIAM ARTHUR WARD

Meditation

I genuinely smile throughout my day.

Action

- I will smile at everyone I see today.

- I will smile to improve my appearance.

- I will smile to feel better and to help others feel better.

When we practice smiling, it becomes a habit. When smiling becomes a habit, it eventually becomes our lifestyle. Living a life of smiling, improves our lives, and some research suggests that it may even extend our lives!

On a scale of 1–10, 10 being highest, how would you rate your ability to smile throughout your day? How will you increase your score?

DAY 25

ADVOCATE FOR OTHERS

"Treat people as if they were what they ought to be and you help them to become what they are capable of being."
—JOHANN WOLFGANG VON GOETHE

Advocate for others. To advocate means to be a voice for someone who has no voice or to support or argue for a cause. Advocates come to the aid of others who are being mistreated.

People who advocate for others cannot stand to see someone treated unfairly or suffering hardship. They simply cannot turn the other way and pretend it is not happening. They often feel an overwhelming compulsion to try to correct perceived wrongs and to encourage others to do the same.

We cannot assume that someone else will address the problems that grieve us. Those of us who have the ability to speak or write passionately in defense of another, or of a cause, or of our ideals, values or beliefs should do it. We can use our communication skills, creativity, imagination, and other strengths to help others to see, to understand, and to become compassionate about the unjust or inequitable realities of which they were previously unaware.

We can each leave our marks on the world by standing up for what we believe is right. Some examples of everyday advocacy include writing an op-ed to a newspaper to express a personal opinion about a subject we care deeply about; standing up to someone who is bullying a child or a compromised person; or speaking to the city council about suggested changes that will make the community safer for all, especially for its most vulnerable residents.

To help others see what we see, we must try to educate others, not argue with them. To make real progress in advocacy, it is important to begin on the common ground of agreement. Approaching someone with a condescending or argumentative attitude will never persuade anyone to see your point of view. However, when we approach others from the perspective of truly trying to help them understand, while trying to understand their thoughts and feelings as well, we can make significant, meaningful progress.

People are also not permanently moved to compassion through manipulation or by physical or emotional force. The real opportunity for transformation happens when advocacy is approached in the context of relationship. When we connect with others in authentic relationships, we are far more likely to listen with the intention to hear and understand the thoughts, feelings, and reasonings of the other person. When we do that, we are more likely to persuade or to at least help others understand why we believe as we do.

The good news is that even when we do not reach agreement, we are in a much better position to understand one another after an emotionally honest exchange of thoughts and feelings. The only way to arrive at this place is to put our relationships first.

> *"Speak up for those who cannot speak for themselves, for the rights of all who are destitute."*
> —Proverbs 31:8

Meditation

I advocate for others and for what I believe is right.

Action

- I will seek to educate others, not to argue.

- I will try to establish relationships before attempting to persuade someone.

- I will always put relationships over agreement.

When we begin to practice relationship-based advocacy for those who are more vulnerable than we are and for our values and beliefs, we are modeling for others how to stand up for what is right while showing respect for others and value for our relationships.

On a scale of 1–10, 10 being highest, how would you rate your ability to advocate for others? How will you increase your score?

DAY 26
TELL THE TRUTH

"Love cannot long survive without truth. Nor is truth really truth unless it is integrated with love."
—MICHAEL O'BRIEN

Tell the truth. No one likes to be lied to, yet, everyone has lied at one time or another. We lied and said the dog ate our homework when in truth, we chose to play instead of doing our assignment. We lied and told the officer we were not speeding when we were going 45-mph in a 35-mph zone. We lied and said we did not feel well when we just wanted to take a day off of work to play.

In our most important asset—our relationships—lies are a death sentence. Good relationships are damaged by our failure to tell the truth, and if enough damage is done, lies will eventually kill them.

There are six basic reasons why people lie. The first is to maintain control of their privacy. They do not want to tell where they really went, what they did, or who they were with because they want to maintain control over their private life.

The second reason is protection of their reputation. When people feel ashamed about something they have done or that has been done to them, they will concoct untrue stories to avoid talking about the shameful truth.

The third reason is self-promotion. People who lie to make themselves look better are the people who photoshop their selfies, agree with others in order to fit in, or exaggerate on their resume to get hired. Sadly, these people do not think they are enough without bolstering themselves with lies.

The fourth reason is avoidance of consequences. These are the kids who lie about breaking their mother's favorite coffee mug to avoid getting in trouble, the people who cheat on their income tax return to avoid paying more taxes, and the significant other who lies about having lunch with an old flame to avoid the damage they think the truth could do to their relationship.

The fifth reason is persuasion. These are the people who lie to get others to buy their product, join them in wrongdoing, or agree with their position. These people will say whatever they think will persuade others to do something that will benefit them.

The sixth reason people lie is because they compartmentalize different parts of their lives in an attempt to protect others. These are often people who deal with confidential or very difficult issues in their lives (such as police officers, mental health professionals, etc.), and they commit the lies of omission to maintain confidentiality or to protect the people they care about from the ugliness they see. In their minds, they are not lying. They believe that they are doing the right thing by not sharing all the information.

Let's take a look at our own lives. Where are we trying to exercise control and why? What are we ashamed of, and isn't it time to let that go? How are we exaggerating to enhance our reputations?

What consequences are we trying to avoid? Who are we trying to persuade and why? If we are compartmentalizing to protect others, do we have a healthy outlet for the truth?

"Can you love people into truth? Absolutely."
—ABBY JOHNSON

Meditation

I tell the truth.

Action

- I will take an honest look at the times I have lied to understand why I did it.

- I will not try to make myself seem better than I am. I am enough.

- I will not lie to persuade someone to do something that I want them to do.

When we begin to live a life of truth, our lives are less complicated, we are happier, and our relationships are better. When we become thoroughly truthful, we are able to help other people choose to live a life of truth.

On a scale of 1–10, 10 being highest, how would you rate your ability to tell the truth? How will you increase your score?

DAY 27
BE AUTHENTIC

"Authenticity is the daily practice of letting go of who we think we're supposed to be and embracing who we are."

—Brené Brown

B e authentic. We all want authenticity. Think about it, you want the diamond you purchase to be real and not a fake. You want your designer handbag to be authentic and not a counterfeit. We want the people closest to us to be real and honest and not phony liars.

Authentic people are real. They have no need to exaggerate to make themselves seem more important or accomplished. They are comfortable with who they are. They are confident in what they know and what they do not know, so they have no reservations about asking questions and learning from others. Because of their comfort and confidence, they are predictable. When you know who they are, you know what they are likely to say and do, which makes being in relationship with them easier than with people who are not authentic.

In a world of copycats and counterfeits, how can we know if someone is authentic?

When we become truly authentic, we naturally gravitate toward people who are authentic. When we are living transparently, we can easily spot a phony. One of the ways we do that is to notice whether the person needs approval from others or is comfortable with him or herself without needing the acceptance of others.

Another tell-tale sign of an inauthentic person is someone who is jealous or envious of others. People who are authentic can be happy for others without being threatened by them. They can wholeheartedly celebrate the achievements or accolades of others because they know their own worth and value. It is not that authentic people do not acknowledge their faults and failings, they do, but they know that their imperfections are balanced by the good character traits, abilities, and talents within themselves.

An authentic person has the courage to follow his or her heart regardless of where the crowd goes. They are able to defend their positions, but often feel no obligation to do so. They feel no compulsion to go with the crowd, to agree with others, or to conform to the trends, beliefs, or values of others. While it may bother an authentic person to be shunned by others, they do not let that diminish their self-worth.

Some examples of ways to identify a truly authentic person are that they hold firmly to their faith even if everyone around them is atheist. They vote their conscience regardless of whether everyone in their life is voting differently. They can passionately express themselves, and they are typically willing to listen to others share from their hearts about opposing opinions. They do not have hidden agendas or play mind games with others because they are not in competition with anyone.

Authentic people tend to leave an indelible mark on everyone within their influence. They are respected, admired, and loved. So, when we become truly authentic people, we will have more of those things in our relationships with the people in our lives.

"Authenticity is about imperfection. And authenticity is a very human quality. To be authentic is to be at peace with your imperfections. The great leaders are not the strongest, they are the ones who are honest about their weaknesses. The great leaders are not the smartest; they are the ones who admit how much they don't know. The great leaders can't do everything; they are the ones who look to others to help them. Great leaders don't see themselves as great; they see themselves as human."
—SIMON SINEK

Meditation

I am authentic.

Action

- I will be real and genuine in every relationship.

- I will live my own conscious and not conform to any group.

- I will never lie or do anything that is inauthentic.

Being authentic is a lifestyle, and when we begin to live it, inauthentic people will stand out to us so that we can choose to help them or avoid them.

On a scale of 1–10, 10 being highest, how would you rate your ability to be authentic? How will you increase your score?

PHYSICAL TOUCH

"I've learned that every day you should reach out and touch someone. People love a warm hug, or just a friendly pat on the back."

—MAYA ANGELOU

Physical touch can be so important in our lives. Can you recall a time as a child when a parent rubbed your shoulders, tousled your hair, or held your hand? Was there ever a time when you and your best childhood friends grabbed each other's pinky? Or what about the first time you held hands with a girl or a boy you liked. All of these types of physical touch can bring back vivid feelings and emotions that we haven't thought about in years. That is the power of physical touch.

To touch someone or to be touched in the right way at the right time can be healing. A warm hug when you are hurting or a hand on your shoulder when you are going through a hard time can mean more than a thousand words could ever mean because touch meets us in a non-verbal place. It can take our emotions back to a time before we had words to express our thoughts and feelings.

Appropriate touch helps us feel more loved and understood. It establishes or reinforces feelings of the strength in our relationships. It can help us navigate through conflict because it communicates that the relationship is more important than winning an argument. The right touch in the right moment can communicate worth and value in a way that nothing else can.

As we incorporate physical touch into our lives, it is important to understand that inappropriate touch can damage our relationships to the degree that appropriate touch can heal. For this reason, we have to be sure that others are comfortable with physical touch before we hug them. There are some people who bristle at physical touch. They may have sensory issues that make physical touch uncomfortable or even unbearable. They may have been hurt by someone and do not want to let anyone close enough to harm them again. There may be cultural meanings to hugs for others of which we are unaware. Still others are very reserved and prefer to maintain ample distance from others. Regardless of the reason, always respect the boundaries of others.

To know how a person feels about physical touch, watch his or her body language. Watch his or her actions. Does the person touch others? If so, chances are they are comfortable with others with whom they are in relationship touching them in appropriate ways. The most obvious way is to simply ask, "May I give you a hug?"

Today's discussion would not be complete without adding that the best hugs (outside of a romantic relationship) are quick side hugs or hugs in which there is space between the people involved. When we follow this guideline, we avoid sending the wrong message or making others feel uncomfortable.

Also, physical touch in the workplace is almost always improper and to be avoided, with the possible exception of the "elbow or fist bump" that has replaced the traditional handshake. Outside of that, it is best if we reserve our physical touch for those with whom we have personal relationships outside of the workplace.

For the people with whom you are closest, always be prepared to hold hands, stroke their hair, put a loving hand on a shoulder, or give a hug. These gifts of affection and the emotions they trigger can stay with others for a lifetime.

"Too often we underestimate the power of a touch."
—LEO BUSCAGLIA

Meditation

I show love through appropriate physical touch.

Action

- I will always be sure that the recipient is comfortable with my gift of physical affection.

- I will be open to the physical touch of others.

- I will never engage in inappropriate physical touch.

Physical affection can be mutually nurturing. Let's intentionally incorporate it into our relationships to give love to ourselves and others.

On a scale of 1–10, 10 being highest, how would you rate your ability to give appropriate physical affection? How will you increase your score?

DAY 29
OFFER HELP

*"Life's most persistent and urgent question
is, 'What are you doing for others?'"*
—MARTIN LUTHER KING, JR.

Offer help. This may sound like a benign, even trite, suggestion on your way to giving and receiving love, but actually, understanding how to offer help to the people in our lives is important because to do so in the wrong way may be misguided and thereby detrimental to our relationships.

Many people will casually mention in conversation something like, "How can I help?" Or at the very end of a conversation, mention an obligatory sounding, "If I can help you, let me know." Although well-meaning, both of these comments can be misguided or mis-timed.

This is not to imply that we should not offer help, but rather than we should do it slightly differently. When we choose the wrong timing for offering help, people often respond by protecting their pride by saying something like, "I'm fine, thanks." The person may not feel comfortable in saying what he or she really needs.

Many people may not have a clear idea of what they need. These people will typically respond with either the "I'm good" message or with a superficial answer such as, "Well, maybe you could pick my mail up while I'm in the hospital." If the person is facing a serious health challenge, there may be far more pressing needs than having his or her mail picked up.

These types of responses are the socially courteous responses that almost automatically fly out of our mouths when we hear a seemingly perfunctory offer of help.

To offer meaningful and relevant help to others, first consider their situation. Think about what you might need if you were in that situation. Then think about what you are able and willing to do for them. Then ask the person if you can have a conversation about how you might be able to help. This will give the person some time to really consider what he or she needs.

When you have the conversation, do not assume that you know what the person needs or even what the person is going through. We rarely have all the details about what someone is going through, and we cannot ever know fully what someone is thinking or feeling. It is important to begin by asking questions and then listening to the person's response. What you think they need may be very different from what they say they need.

If you are listening with the intention to really hear and learn, you may learn things about the person that you did not know. Providing a sincere offer to provide meaningful help to someone can help to strengthen a relationship. Following through on what you offer to do can strengthen it exponentially.

After you have heard what the person shares about his or her needs, be specific about what you offer to do. Only offer what you are confident that you can follow through with, and then be sure to do what you agree to do.

"The purpose of human life is to serve, and to show compassion and the will to help others."
—ALBERT SCHWEITZER

Meditation

I listen to others and offer relevant help.

Action

- I will pay attention to the people in my life to notice when I think they may need help.

- I will ask to have conversations about offering help.

- I will listen to what others need before offering help.

When we offer valuable help to others at times in their lives when they truly need it, we strengthen our relationships. Although we never offer help in exchange for what others can do for us, when we provide help to others in their time of need, it is more likely that others will be there for us when we need help.

On a scale of 1–10, 10 being highest, how would you rate your ability to offer help? How will you increase your score?

DAY 30
SERVE OTHERS

"Everybody can be great...because anybody can serve. You don't have to have a college degree to serve. You don't have to make your subject and verb agree to serve. You only need a heart full of grace. A soul generated by love."

—MARTIN LUTHER KING, JR.

Serve others. The secret to a meaningful life that is full of love is to give ourselves away in service to others.

It may seem counterintuitive to think that by serving others, we will bring love into our lives, but that is exactly what happens. When we adopt the mindset of a desire to serve others, we become more likable, more worthy of respect and of admiration. If we live consistently like this, we develop a lifestyle that fills our lives with love.

Of course, we do not seek to serve others to earn these things, but this is the natural outgrowth of a life of service to others.

Meaning and purpose is found in service to others because when we serve, we engage our natural talents and abilities, our genuine personality traits, and our strongest character traits. We are our most authentic when we are serving others by doing what comes naturally to us. For example, if we are an empathetic person who is a naturally good listener, serving by listening to someone when they need a friend helps the other person while meeting a need in us. If we are talented at fixing things, serving someone by making a minor repair helps the other person and makes us feel good.

Serving others gives us practical ways to incorporate social connections into our lives. Doing what we can for others and being willing to receive help from others establishes relationship connections for us that can enhance the lives of everyone involved.

People who live lives of service are often more successful in the workplace and in the community.

They do not demand their own way and are happy to listen to the ideas and suggestions of others. They know that the contributions of others do not diminish their own, but rather contribute to the greater good. They tend to be confident without an overblown ego. Consequently, they make good leaders. In fact, people who follow the principles of what is commonly referred to as "servant leadership," are known for their empathy, their genuine concern for others, their listening skills, and their ability to gain cooperation of others.

People who serve others seek to educate, not to manipulate others to come around to their way of thinking. They feel purposeful and they naturally help others to feel that way because they notice the skills, talents, and positive character traits of the people around them.

Some people mistake serving others for weakness. These are the people who also confuse kindness with weakness. Service to others actually indicates the opposite of weakness. It requires strength of character and personality and con- fidence in self to create a lifestyle of service to others.

"Successful people are always looking for opportunities to help others.

Unsuccessful people are always asking, 'What's in it for me?'"
—Brian Tracy

Meditation

I live in service to others.

Action

- I will look for ways to serve others.

- I will think of the ways that I am most comfortable serving others.

- I will not expect anything in return for my service to others.

When we live a life of service, we enrich our lives in ways that we may not even be able to imagine. We attract good people into our lives. We become happier, more fulfilled, and more loving of ourselves and others.

On a scale of 1–10, 10 being highest, how would you rate your ability to serve others? How will you increase your score?

CONCLUSION

"Since love grows within you, so beauty grows. For love is the beauty of the soul."
—SAINT AUGUSTINE

Over these past 30 days, you have learned how to give and receive love in the most practical and in the most profound of ways. Now that you have practiced love for these past 30 days, do you see yourself ever going back? If you have really applied these ideas, you will never again want to live a life that is not focused on giving and receiving love, which is the most meaningful thing we can do in this life.

Love gives us hope.

Love gives us meaning.

Love enriches our lives.

Love inspires us to reach for our goals.

Love gives us energy.

Love empowers us to keep going.

Love promotes emotional wellbeing.

Love reduces anxiety, worry, and fear.

Love lifts our mood.

Love makes us happy.

Love builds our self-esteem.

Love sparks our creativity.

Love helps us grow.

Love empowers us to be more loving.

Love validates our worth.

You are one-of-a-kind in all the world, in all of humanity, for all time. You are awesome, in the truest sense of that word. You are awe-inspiring. As you learn that, and absorb it, and embrace it, you will get better and better at living a life of love.

May you find that repeating these acts of love every day for the rest of your life, fills your life with true, unconditional, love.

"To be successful is to be helpful, caring and constructive, to make everything and everyone you touch a little bit better."
—Norman Vincent Peale

ABOUT THE AUTHOR

Rhonda Sciortino is an author, speaker, business owner, and founder of Successful Survivors Foundation, an educational non-profit organization that exists to help survivors of trauma create successful lives. Rhonda is also the national champion of the LOVE IS ACTION COMMUNITY INITIATIVE.

She is a successful survivor of child abuse and is a passionate advocate for children who have been abandoned, neglected, abused, and/or trafficked.

To help people who come from hard places, Rhonda created the Your Real Success program. Through it, she helps others mine the lessons out of what they have been through, and apply those lessons (character traits, learned abilities, and coping skills) to create personal and professional success.

Rhonda lives with her husband Nick and rescue dog, Lucky. Their daughter, son-in-love, and grandchildren are the joys of their lives.

Visit www.rhonda.org for more information.

ALSO BY
RHONDA SCIORTINO

The Prayer That Covers It All: Gain a deep but simple understanding of the Lord's Prayer

Keys to Answered Prayer: What Does God's Word Say About Answered Prayer?